Praise for The Highest Light Teachings

The remarkable teachings Tony offers us in this work have the power to transform your life and to heal our world! This information has come to us at exactly the right time and I encourage you to buy this book today!

Richard Ross,
Developer, Emotional Freedom & Healing Modalities
Ashland, Oregon
www.emotionalfreedom.com

Tony Burroughs lights up our hearts with his Highest Light Teachings. Our often cold and dark contemporary world needs the gentle light and ancient wisdom of his spirit to show us the way. This book offers a distinctive view of human purpose, as well as offering comfort, and a call for all of us to live a higher order life at this time in history.

Bonnie Taulere MS, MCC
President, Quality of Life Coaching Services, Inc
Sarasota, Florida
www.qualityoflifecoaching.com

If you're ready to claim your own power and live your life at the highest levels, then The Highest Light Teachings is one book you'll want to read and reread. This simple book contains profound truths that will help free you from your illusions and see yourself as the magnificence you truly are.

Jim Donovan
Author, <u>Reclaim Your Life</u>
Doylestown, Pennsylvania
www.jimdonovan.com

The Highest Light Teachings

Copyright © 2002 by Tony Burroughs
All Rights Reserved
Printed in the United States of America
First Printing: June 2002
ISBN: 0-9654288-4-2
Cover Graphics by Tony Burroughs
Cover Photo thanks to NASA

This book is dedicated to Lee Ching
Great Commander, Savior, brother, friend

A special thanks to Intenders of the Highest Good and likehearted groups everywhere who are expressing their gratitudes and intentions, becoming empowered, and lighting the way for so many others to follow. Likewise, my gratitude also runs deep for four very good friends. Without their gifts of true friendship, love and guidance, this book would not be.

Michele Liberman sat down with me not long ago and suggested that I write down my ideas. She was the spark on that day, as she is in all of my days. I love you, Michele.

Tina Stober gave me the greatest of gifts. She introduced me to my Higher Self. I can't imagine my life without her in it. May God always bless you, Tina, as you have blessed me.

Betsy Whitney is the most inspiring person I've ever met. She gave me new sight and, whenever I fall asleep to it, she always wakes me up. Mahalo nui kealoha, Bets.

Connie Ritchey is my true sister in my soul. Her heart is so pure and gentle, that to be in her presence is just like being with an angel. Connie, you are the highest light.

The ideas in this book are the views of the author only. They are not, in any way, meant to represent the personal beliefs of others who are also Intenders of the Highest Good.

The Highest Light Teachings

Tony Burroughs

Dolphin Press
Hilo, Hawaii

-Table of Contents-

Introduction

I. Beginning To Glow

Seeing Ourself in our Highest Light
1. You've Never Made a Mistake
2. You're Doing It To You
3. Learning To Discern
4. Giving The Universe More Leeway
5. Tapping into Your Higher Self
6. Be Your Own Drummer
7. Finding Your Calling
8. Healing Ourselves

II. Turning Up The Brightness

Seeing Others in their Highest Light
1. Taking Charge
2. Starting Up An Isness Business
3. Suffering Isn't Necessary
4. Granting A Full Pardon
5. The Story of Another Christ
6. Healing Others

III. Lighting Up The Earth

Seeing Our World in its Highest Light
1. Our Next Step Together
2. Peace Must Take Precedence
3. The Good Side
4. Live Wires Make Great Connections
5. The Highest Light Party
6. Healing Our World

IV. The Light Of A Thousand Suns

Seeing The Universe in its Highest Light

-Introduction -

Much like life itself, this little booklet begins and ends with Oneness. Envision for a moment, if you will, a time before you were born. You floated about effortlessly in a singular limitless substance. You knew that all things were connected and, therefore, you - and everything else - were part and parcel of All That Is. A sublime comfort zone surrounded you and penetrated into your whole world. You were alive, but without a solid, breathing body to identify with - able to know anything, be everything, create at will.

Then, somewhere along the line, you decided to have some fun and incarnate into a body - and before you knew it, certain rules and resistances became apparent. Life on Earth, though abundant with rich feelings and experiences, had its risks. A wide variety of illusions and games presented themselves and you said to yourself, "This looks interesting! I think I'll play this game for awhile. Why not? Everybody else is playing it. When the time comes for me to set aside this silly amusement and return to the way I felt as a child, it won't be any problem."

So you jumped in with both feet, started giving names to everything around you (including yourself), agreed that a great many artificial boundaries were real, created false identities and relationships, arbitrarily gave power to other people which allowed them to control you, began making judgments, and so forth. Life went on and as the years passed, you became more and more enmeshed in your illusions. When the time arrived for you to set aside all your games and dramas, it turned out that it wasn't so easy. You'd been heavily programmed and had developed habits that didn't want to go away.

Such is the challenge that faces most people today. They're playing games; some taking life less seriously, while others are passionately putting everything they have on the line. In both instances, however, most people have long forgotten the moment when they chose to start playing. Most are lost in the dramas.

The purpose of these teachings is to show you a way out, to free you from your own games and illusions so that you can start to see yourself in your highest light. Let us now begin with the first premise in this booklet: You've never made a mistake.

I.
- Beginning To Glow -
Seeing Yourself in Your Highest Light

You've Never Made A Mistake

Perhaps one of the greatest challenges that faces the average person today is believing in their own self-worth. From the time we were small children, our view of our highest light has been undermined. It's pretty easy to recall past experiences where we've been told that we were less than we thought we were or that we'd made a mistake. Our teachers, parents, peers, the TV, and all sorts of sources have, either consciously or unconsciously, talked us into limiting ourselves. Over a lifetime, our power was slowly but steadily stripped away from us. But now all of that is changing.

These teachings emphasize that you've never made a mistake. When the incident occured where you thought you'd made a mistake, it wasn't until after the incident was over that you gleaned the knowledge from it. While the incident was still in progress, you were only operating on the basis of the best information that you had at the time. In truth, you couldn't have known any better and, therefore, there was no reason for you to beat yourself up about it. You were presented with a lesson, but no mistake was made.

Learning a lesson and making a mistake are two entirely different things. Lessons don't carry the same feelings as mistakes. There's no guilt attached to our lessons, but mistakes imply that we've done something wrong. Those who view life from a higher perspective know that they've never done anything wrong. Everything just happens and it doesn't serve us to place moral judgments on any events that occur in our lives. The concept of right and wrong is simply another illusion that doesn't exist for us unless we nourish it. We can choose to plead "not guilty" to all of the menacing "should haves" that charge us with wrongdoing. *In our mind, we can assert that everything is all right regardless of what others may say,* and, in doing so, we return to the innocence we were born with.

One of the main themes that runs throughout these pages is that we always have a choice as to which thoughts we put our attention on. More importantly, since we are becoming more aware each day that our thoughts create our future, it becomes a matter of reprogramming our thoughts so that we choose the ones that serve us and discard the ones that don't serve us. This is the first step in walking a new path - a path that leads to happiness, a grand view of ourselves, and a life lived to its fullest.

There are many who are choosing to walk this path now. It doesn't involve any special training or journeys to sacred sites. You can do it where you sit or stand at any given moment. Tell yourself that you are a grand and glorious being, placed here on this beautiful Earth to reap all of the rewards that are put before you. Tell yourself, everyday, that you are deserving of all of the gifts and abundance that life has to offer. Tell yourself that you are perfect, just the way you are, and that you have the same powers and potentials that every other man and woman has.

And then just be open to receive.

The laws of manifestation work for everyone. If you keep your thoughts on your strengths, you will become strong. If you know that you are a good and kind person who deserves the very best in life, you will quickly see your most wondrous dreams materialize before your eyes. As sure as creation follows thought, you will, one day, find yourself lifted up - exalted - to a place that's been waiting there for you all along. You'll see yourself clearly as the magnificent being that you truly are.

If, for some reason, you begin to give in to your fears or doubts, remember that there are two sides to every thought. You always have the choice of calling forth the other half of your thought - your positive thought.

You always have the option of seeing yourself in your highest light.

*How much greater you are
than you think you are*

You're Doing It To You

One of the main ingredients to a happy life is knowing that you're running the show. Nobody else is doing it to you; you're doing it all to yourself. Wouldn't it be nice if everyone knew this and began to take responsibility for their actions? You'd be able to count on them. If you were working with them and they changed their mind or couldn't show up, they'd call and let you know. You wouldn't have to be concerned that you'd been lied to or that the job would be disrupted. Life would run smoothly because there wouldn't be any blame game going on.

You know how the blame game goes. Something goes awry, and instead of acknowledging that he's had any part in the incident, the blamer immediately says, "I didn't do it" or "It wasn't me". He shifts the blame for his actions to someone else and is less apt to tell the truth because he's afraid you'll be mad, like his father or third grade principal was. He'd rather avoid having his ego stepped on than face his fears. Granted, it takes courage to be responsible, but once you do, you'll never want to go back to your old ways. You'll breathe easier because you're not carrying around all of the heavy burdens that weigh fearful people down. And you won't have to keep track of a string of lies because you're willing to tell the truth.

So few people nowadays have true integrity and are willing to stand up and say "I did it. I'll take full responsibility for what went on in my life." When this does happen, it's like a rare polished gem that shines from the midst of a bunch of pebbles. What a joy to behold - a totally responsible person who is unafraid to speak the truth. And truth it is, indeed. *For in every event in which we're involved, it is always we who make the choice to take part beforehand.* Whether we're conscious of our previous decisions or not doesn't lessen the fact that that's the way things work.

Let's take another example to bring this concept closer to home. Suppose, one bright and sunny morning, you were having breakfast when the thought crossed your mind that you needed some things at the grocery store. In short order, you finished your eggs and toast, grabbed your coat, and hurried off to the local Piggly-Wiggly. Shopping took about 20 minutes and after you loaded your bags of groceries into the trunk of your car, you backed right smack dab into the rear bumper of an SUV. Nobody was hurt, but when you got out to inspect the damage, the other driver screamed at you and you screamed back. Both of you claimed that the other one was to blame.

The truth, however, is that both of you were responsible. Both of you decided to go to the grocery store.

Both of you made the choice to be in that parking lot on that sunny morning. No one forced either one of you to go to the market. You freely decided on your own, knowing that anything could happen along the way. The question is: Can you see that these thoughts came to you long before the accident? And therefore, can you stop blaming others and take full responsibility for your actions?

As we steadily monitor our thoughts and become more and more truthful with ourselves, we'll find that we are the primary cause of all that goes on in our life. We'll see that our thoughts are creating our world and that no one else is holding a whip over us telling us which thoughts to think and act on. The nice thing about all this is that when we decide to quit playing the blame game and be responsible, the illusion of separation dissolves because there are no longer any perpetrators or victims. Now we're free to explore our Oneness with everything and everybody else. We're free to shine our highest light.

Such freedom is available to all of us. All we have to do is remember that we're in charge of our own behavior, and that we always have a choice. No one else is doing it to us. We're doing it all to ourselves.

The reality that you create is up to you

Learning To Discern

Many people make their decisions from their solar plexus. That's where our "wants" are. We feel a tug in our midsection, and our emotions take over from there. Frequently, however, things don't turn out the way we'd like, and that's because our emotional feelings are not very dependable guides. Everything would have been much better for us if we'd first consulted with our two higher, more reliable advisors - our head and our heart.

It helps us immeasurably to parade our choices past our mind before we make a decision. Our mind accesses past events and bids us to learn from our experiences. If we had previously gone down a challenging path, it's likely that our mind will sound an alarm that signals us to beware, lest we repeat the same experience.

Likewise, our imagination is good at showing us potential futures. It can project a myriad of outcomes, but we must ask ourselves if each outcome is apt to take us closer to or farther away from our goals in life? Does this particular choice serve our highest and best good or not?

Left to itself, our mind will answer these and many other questions sufficiently, except for one small detail. Unless we're living at the level of mastery, our egos tend to play tricks on us. We tell ourselves lies - and then act upon those lies as if they were everlasting truths. Until we're in total alignment with our highest good, our mind, like our lower emotions, can only serve to provide us with rough guidelines. It doesn't give us the last word.

That's where the heart comes in. After we have carefully reflected on our past and then pictured all possible outcomes, we go to the source of all wisdom - our heart. Discernment's final test asks us how we feel in our heart about the choices that are available to us. The Carlos Casteneda/don Juan books said it best. When Carlos, the apprentice, asked don Juan, the old Indian sorcerer, which is the best path to follow, don Juan told him to follow the path that has a heart. In this instance, the old sorcerer was referring to spiritual paths in general. But the same answer could easily hold true for all decisions we make. Follow your heart. Those whose lives flow, like a clear mountain stream running smoothly downhill, discern from the center of their heart. For that is where we touch all that is true and good.

*Go forth with love
and all is added unto you*

Giving The Universe More Leeway

At one time or another, all of us have worked with someone who had the habit of setting predetermined time limits as to when the job you were doing together would be finished. They would start out the morning by saying that your work would be done by 4:00 pm and, after that, it'd be Miller time. As is often the case, the work proceeded okay for awhile, but invariably some interruption or unforeseen circumstances arose - it rained, you ran out of some widgets you needed, or someone didn't show up on time.

All of a sudden, your co-worker who wanted to be finished by 4 was in a tizzy. He was working faster, complaining louder, pushing everyone else a little harder. In short, he was beginning to struggle. As the day wore on, and his goals clearly weren't going to be met, his whole countenance and behavior changed because he couldn't meet his deadline.

And all of this happened because he set up those predetermined goals in the morning. His predeterminations didn't make the work go any easier. In fact, they were disruptive. If he hadn't set up his goals, the work would have proceeded normally. When you sat back later and reflected on it all, you could see that the exact amount of work that got done that day was all that could have been done, and your co-worker's expectations didn't change a thing - except that the job wasn't as much fun because of his pushing and complaining.

This is just one example of how our expectations can be a challenge for us. In this particular instance, time parameters were the culprit; however, we could just as easily have been expecting how far we were going to travel, what someone was going to look like, where something was going to come from, and so on. *The symbols are many, but the function is always the same - when we expect something specific, we set ourselves up for a loss.*

The standard rule of thumb is that it's okay to set goals. Indeed, it's part of the creative process. But it doesn't serve us to make predeterminations of when, how, or with whom our goals will manifest. In truth, we can never really know how long something is going to take. Nor can we really be sure how anything will find its way to us. We unduly limit ourselves when we envision that our creations are coming to us through specific, predetermined channels. In essence, we're short-circuiting the magical workings of the Universe.

We must always remember that the Universe is unlimited. It can find an infinite number of ways to be creative. We may expect, for example, that in order to have a car, we need to go out and get a job, qualify for a loan, make a down payment, and then work hard each day to pay off our debt. If this is what we believe we need to do in order to have the car, then that is how the car will come to us.

The Universe, in its boundless wisdom, might do things a little differently. It might arrange for you to win the car in a raffle, or have a good friend give you the car. At the same time, if you're completely trusting and are willing to provide the Universe with a little more leeway, you might even receive a vehicle more suitable for your long-range purposes, like a van, or a full-sized SUV.

We open the door to the miraculous when we give the Universe a little more room to maneuver. By saying something like, "I know that you know what is better for me than I know for myself. I ask that you bring me the perfect vehicle for my purposes in life. I am open to receive it freely and effortlessly from both expected and unexpected sources", we make everything easier for ourselves. We discover that the Universe is user-friendly, and that we might as well get used to going directly to the fountainhead.

After all, it all comes from the same Source anyway.

When man remembers his spiritual connection to All That Is, he lives in a most joyous state wherever he is, whatever he is doing

Tapping Into Your Higher Self

We live in a time, according to the Mayans, when the adage "Time is money" defines our lifestyle. Our highest priorities revolve around money - its gathering, its hoarding, its spending. None but those who deliberately choose to isolate themselves from civilization are untouched by money's all-pervading power. And, all too often, human creativity is left to sit on the back burner while the lure of money takes precedence in our lives.

Fortunately for us, times are changing and so are our values. As we become less and less enamored with the current paradigm and all of its demands, we seek alternatives that will bring us greater satisfaction in life. "Time is money" is gradually being replaced by "Time is art", and creativity is surfacing within many who previously thought themselves to be too busy or not talented enough to be imaginative. Our untapped potentials are expanding and bringing with them a much richer level of experience. Furthermore, it's not only we as individuals who are growing and blossoming as this shift occurs, but humanity as a whole profits by the abundance of new writings, paintings, sculptures, inventions, and so forth. What was once fascinating in black and white now colors our world and excites our senses in ways we never expected. Our enhanced creativity shows us that we are evolving.

For those who would like to tap into their creative powers, a few guidelines are helpful. One formula that has worked for many suggests that we follow four steps. The first step, like the Nike commercial says, is "Just do it". This means that we set all other things aside and go to work. If we are a writer, we go to a quiet place, pick up a pen and paper or sit at the keyboard, and write. If we are a sculptor, we need to pick up a hammer and chisel and start chipping away. It may sound simplistic to mention this, but, if we don't make the first move, then nothing will ever happen. We must roll up our sleeves and go to work.

Second, it serves us to calm ourselves. Before you begin your work, close your eyes for a moment, take a few deep breaths and relax. Let go of the cares and concerns of the day and wait until they are replaced by an inner peace. Some people go into a mild trancelike state, while others simply relax. It doesn't matter how you do it.

The next step is to make a short intention which calls forth the highest good. If you're a writer, for example, say aloud, *"I intend that everything needing to be known is known here and now; that all of my words are clear, precise and uplifting; that I am guided, guarded and protected during this entire process; and that all of my writings serve the highest and best good of the Universe, myself, and everyone concerned. So be it and so it is."*

An intention/invocation like this insures that only the highest good will come through. It creates a firm connection between us and our Higher Self, which is where our most inspired creative abilities reside.

Finally, we need to relinquish the temptation to think. All of our thinking and mental preparation must have already taken place prior to the actual act of creation. It's alright to plan and explore all avenues within our imagination before we approach our work, but, once the work begins, thinking will only get in the way. All great creative genius comes when we stop thinking and get into the spontaneous flow of the creative process itself. You'll know when you're in this flow because time will disappear - hours go by unnoticed - as you're magically guided to write the next line or place your next brush stroke. It's as if the Infinite Wisdom of the Universe comes through you and moves your hand. All you have to do is stay receptive and avoid the temptation to start thinking.

The creative process is one of the most enjoyable things you can do. When you're in the midst of it, you'll feel like you're riding in the curl of a perfect wave that wraps itself around you, powerfully, yet with such grace and beauty as to render you in awe of its magic. And when you're finished, it delivers you up onto the shore where you take a breather and turn around to see what you have done. In that sweet moment of exhilaration, you savor the exquisite feeling of satisfaction that pulses through your entire body. Your every cell is alive and humming.

Chances are you'll want to swim right back out and do it all again.

Your purpose is to be revealed to you
so that you can spread your wings and
cover this Earth with that which is your creation

Be Your Own Drummer

A few years back, the Matrix think-tankers published an article that said that the powers-that-be in our world are using three primary subliminal messages in the mainstream media. The purpose of these messages is to keep people under their thumbs, controlled, and acting like sheep who mindlessly follow each other around. The three subliminals are: *conform, consume, and die.*

It's obvious that it doesn't serve us to manifest any of these suggestions, but for the time being we will only concern ourselves with becoming more conscious of the first subliminal - *conform*. We do this because it's the easiest one to eliminate from our present behavior patterns.

From the time that we were small children, we've been taught to mind our manners and to be like everybody else. We're told that it's respectful of others to practice certain courtesies, and that's fine, as long as we don't become slaves to what other people think or say about us. Taken too far, our conformity keeps us living in a subtle, but very real, state of fear. We become afraid of acting differently than everyone else around us. Even when our heart tells us to do something one way, our social consciousness screams out to do it another way, lest we draw too much attention to ourselves. And all too often, our fear wins out.

To experience your highest light, you must break the mold. You must do things not as others do, but as your heart bids you to do. Put on your old comfortable, raggedy clothes and take a walk around the park; whisper to a flower in your backyard; get up at four in the morning and go out and take a look at the pre-dawn skies. There are those who might contend that you're ready for the loony bin. But they'll be the ones who are missing out on some of the finest experiences in life. They'll stay under the thumb, albeit unconsciously, of others who would control their every word and deed. While you, in your newfound wisdom, will begin to walk this Earth freely and fearlessly, without a care in the world.

Know that there will most certainly be times when you'll feel the pressure to conform from those all around you. Just remember, in these moments, that it is you, not them, who gets to sing as you amble through the beautiful park. It is you, not them, who hears the joy in the voice of the flower as she whispers her innermost secrets back unto you. And it is you, not them, who receives loving guidance from the morning star as she breaks the horizon at dawn.

*Look within
and see what will give you the most joy*

Finding Your Calling

Being of service often conjures up images of spending our time doing selfless, but unenjoyable tasks day after day, month after month, for years on end. We've been led to believe that in order to serve God or mankind, we must leave our comfortable lifestyle and become an ascetic who grits their teeth and bears the pain of working at a job that's no fun. Our rewards are in Heaven, we're told, and it doesn't matter if we have to go through Hell to get there. With this grim outlook, it's no wonder that many shun the idea of living a life devoted to service and opt in favor of "the good life".

As with so many illusions that have been passed down to us for eons, this one only tells the unempowered side of the story. The truth bids us to remember that we can have it all. We can have our cake and eat it too. *It's entirely possible to combine what is helpful to others with that which is enjoyable to ourselves.* The Buddhists call it living our dharma, while in the West we know it best as recognizing and following our calling.

You know when you're following your calling. Everything fits snugly into place. Synchronistic events are everyday fare. Life gets easy. When you're truly living in service, all of the guesswork is removed from your life. You're always in the right place at the right time. You feel different because your body is carrying a higher frequency that attracts others to you. The people you're supposed to be working with always show up, as if by magic. Your whole world becomes a delight to live in because you're committed to doing the work that your soul calls you to do.

Some may avoid their calling, and it's easy to tell who they are. They're struggling or beset by obstacles. They're complaining about feeling stuck and not knowing what to do about it. Fortunately, the Universe is also working on their behalf, even if it doesn't seem like it. It continues to present them with opportunities until they pick one that aligns them with their life's purpose.

And that's when everything changes. Your challenges

turn into gifts. Rewards are not deferred until a later date, but delivered freely in the here and now. You feel a great transformation churning inside of you and, at the same time, worldly abundance that was once elusive steps forward and introduces itself.

Now you know that you've settled into your highest destiny, your highest calling. You're suddenly at peace. You're surrounded by people who are grateful to you because you have helped them. You see it in their eyes. You feel it in their hearts. Your life is good because you've remembered what you came here to do.

It's clear that many of us are realizing that we made an agreement before we came into these bodies, that we would come together at a certain time in order to bring light and love onto this planet and to usher in a golden age. Some have forgotten and some just have a feeling, like an inkling of a long-lost dream, that there really is a reason for us to be here now.

In either case, on one level or another, we are all experiencing a movement toward looking at life from the perspective of the soul and the soul group - a perspective of having made agreements and arrangements to come here and meet together with other souls and soul groups - and then join together - so that we can assist in raising the vibration of this planet.

This is what is being remembered at this time; and it is this movement which will, in fact, bring the golden age into manifestation.

Healing Ourselves

Seeing yourself in your highest light is the foundation by which true healing can come to you. That's how the Christ did it. In his mind, he saw everyone he helped, including himself, already living in their highest light - healed, healthy, happy, and whole. Then he petitioned his Father to take over from there.

Our possibilities are limitless. We can all do as the Christ did. Once we set aside all of our old, programmed views of who we are and how we project ourselves out to the world, the door to the miraculous opens. We can take on a new shape, our inner anatomy can return to full health, our spirit can shine.

Healing is always there for everyone, but it's important to understand that many have been completely healed and then reverted back to ill health because they've allowed their old points of view to win out. Our challenge is to hold a vision of ourselves in our highest light indefinitely. A good example of this has to do with a woman who journeyed to see a Native American shaman who specialized in healing. This man had the gift of being able to hold the light for others during times when they were unable to hold it for themselves. Due to his efforts, she was, in fact, restored to optimal health, but, upon arriving home, she hurried to visit her local physician who made a cursory examination and diagnosed that some of her disease symptoms still remained. In believing her physician's diagnosis, she set the wheels in motion for her body to weaken. Had she not given him authority to reinforce her old viewpoints, and had she been able to hold onto the belief in her own wellness, she would have remained as healthy as she was when she left the shaman's tepee.

In learning to see ourselves in our highest light, we must begin to trust in our own authority. This does not mean that we should refrain from seeking help in times of distress - for we must take the course of action that we believe will work. It simply means that it does not serve us to seek outside of ourselves for *reinforcement* of our ills. To the same extent, it is never a good idea to believe that we suffer from a condition that has a medically sanctioned name. The naming of diseases only furthers the spread of sickness because, if we give credence to the disease's name, our subconscious will begin to align itself with the symptoms associated with the disease, and our body, in its all-pervading wisdom, will follow. Indeed, when we accept the name, we are reinforcing our illness by allowing a lesser vision to manifest.

As in all things, our thoughts are what's important. Our body will do what they tell it to do. To the extent that we are able to hold an image of ourselves in a state of perfect health, that is the exact degree to which we will be healed. Likewise, when we are capable of holding a vision of ourselves in our highest light indefinitely, nothing distressful can touch us.

By your thought, shall you be well

II.
- Turning Up The Brightness -
Seeing Others In Their Highest Light

Taking Charge

You know how a battery, like the one in your car, works. It's a storage device that can hold a certain amount of charge - but if you keep adding more charge to it, it will either begin to leak or explode. We human beings work in much the same way; the charge, however, is initially held in our solar plexus and when we get overloaded, we need to find a release, lest we begin to leak our emotional charge out on others - or worse yet, explode in anger at those around us.

Of course, in reality, people are not meant to be storage batteries at all, but perfectly designed transformers. We're at our best when we take in energy, see our life experiences in their highest light (which transforms the energy into a higher frequency), then let it flow out of us creatively. We're able to use our emotional charge to enhance our creativity. It's the power we pour into our work.

Unfortunately, a great many people today do not function near peak efficiency. Because many of their wants go unfulfilled, they find themselves overloaded with charge. These unresolved emotions tend to leak out in the form of negative responses, making them angry, hateful, sorrowful or sick. Those who haven't found a creative outlet for their charge or cannot easily express their emotions often seem like a powder keg ready to ignite at a moment's notice.

Many find an outlet for their negative charge in casual conversation. You can easily recognize these people because they always seem to have a burning issue or problem to talk about. Typically, they would like nothing better than to make their problems your problems and thereby soothe themselves by transferring their negative charge onto you. Afterwards, they generally walk away feeling better, but you walk away feeling like you've been dumped on.

The scene described above takes place all too frequently, but now, things are changing. People are becoming more conscious, and they want to find a way to serve their friends and neighbors without taking on any of their negative charge. For those whose hearts are open, we humbly offer a suggestion: When you envision your friends in their highest light, you automatically shield yourself from harm - and, at the same time, you also create a thoughtform that will help them immensely.

Let's set up a scenario so you can see how this works. You're talking casually with a new acquaintance and suddenly she begins to tell you all about an unusually intense drama that's going on in her life. As she begins to go into more and more detail, you feel a tightening in your gut that wasn't there moments before. Normally, you'd like to commiserate, but now that you've heard about The Highest Light Teachings, you've decided to do something new.

First of all, you're going to withhold any agreement concerning her problems. When she looks at you to agree, you simply utter a flat, noncommittal "Oh" or "Hmmm". You're not nodding your head, even slightly, or saying "Yes". You know that if you were to align with her problems, you'd only be giving power to them - and then you'd open yourself up to take on her charge.

Secondly, you would ground yourself by whatever means you prefer. Some people like to make sure that their feet are flat on the floor, while others envision a pillar of light extending from their body to the center of the Earth. It doesn't matter how you ground yourself, as long as you do it.

And finally, while the social part of you is listening intently to your new friend, you'd shift your awareness to your mind's eye where you'd picture your friend in her highest light. From that vantage point, she is magically relieved of all burdens and surrounded in Universal Love. Her dramas have disappeared and have been replaced by a joy that she hasn't felt since childhood. You'd hold her in that light, no matter what, for as long as you can. When she notices that you've kept your composure throughout the entire conversation, she'll probably want to know how you've managed to stay so upbeat (in comparison to her other friends who usually look pretty ragged by the time she's done with them).

Then you can tell her that it will help her the most if she would spend some time seeing herself free, happy and comforted - just as you've been seeing her. Tell her that her thoughts have a direct effect on her well-being and that she can choose, at anytime, to envision herself living in her highest light.

This method is what works. When you use it, you will find that you have not added fuel to the flames of your friend's melodramatic fires. Nor will you walk away from the conversation feeling drained, with your gut tied in knots. Instead, you will have offered a positive, creative solution to your friend and set an example that acts like a seed that may one day sprout open, grow, and reach upwards toward the light - The Highest Light.

In order for you to see things from a higher ground, you must learn to detach from suffering and drama. The faster you can learn to do whatever it takes to lift yourself up and out of dramatic situations, the better it will be for you and for all those around you. If you need to go out the door and shut it behind you and say, "I'm not going back there for a day or two," then do that. If you're in a situation at work where you're feeling really drained and you need to regenerate, go out into Nature. Nature is there for you. It is filled with vital life and energy. Avail yourself of it. It is your birthright, as a human being, to be with the trees, the wind, the sun and the rain. These things add unto you. They regenerate you. They recreate you.

Starting Up An Isness Business

Judgment is like a double-edged sword - as you judge others, you judge yourself. And, at the same time, you set yourself up for experiences that you might not like. The evolutionary acceleration that all of us are going through at this time insures that we must experience lessons that take us to our next step.

For example, many of us have recently come to the realization that when we make a judgment of someone else, we must be prepared to want something from that person in the near future. There is an old story that brings this truth into focus.

It says that, one cloudy day, you might be walking through a city and pass a begger on the street. His clothes are tattered, his hands and face dirty, his smell sour. In all respects, his appearance represents all that is repulsive to you - and yet . . . he may have something that you want.

The Universe has mysterious, but effective ways of teaching us our lessons. Another old adage says: We become just like those we oppose. This knowledge by itself should be enough to cause us to reevaluate our behavior. For who would choose to live out the experiences of the one they judge? And who, in fact, suffers the most from a judgment made?

Love steps aside every time a judgment is levied, while judgment's shadow comes back to haunt and to teach us the ultimate lesson: That the judgment of others is a judgment upon oneself.

The question then arises: How do we stop a lifelong habit of making judgments, even as it is being done hundreds of times a day by those all around us? First, when the urge to judge surfaces, we can take a couple of deep breaths and remind ourself that judgment-making is not without its drawbacks. We can ask ourself if we would truly want to walk in the other person's footsteps, for that is surely what we can expect from our judging.

Second, we can teach ourselves to remain in a state of Is-ness. Is-ness is where there is no good or bad, no right or wrong, no better or worse. Everything just IS. This great truth enables us to suspend all subjective labels that we put on things. And it protects us from having to go through experiences that are unwanted.

Third, we can begin to understand that there is a big difference between our judgments and our preferences. It serves us to discern that we may prefer chocolate, but that it is not bad when another person prefers vanilla. We can allow others their fullest form of expression, understanding that their preferences may be different than ours, but that both are valid. We need not pass scrutiny on another because he or she prefers something that may not fit us well. *We choose for them whatever makes them happy.*

Fourth and most important, instead of passing judgment on others, we can see them in their highest light. This is what will help them the most. It is time we realized that we are actually harming one another by making constant judgments. If we really want to begin to be helpful to our fellow human beings, we must stop reinforcing their lowest form of expression and start lifting them up. When we see them at their best, living their life to the fullest, we take the first step toward loving them. That's what makes the miracles happen.

For love has something in common with judgment. We always get back what we put out.

See the Essence of Divinity in every person

Suffering Isn't Necessary

We never need to hesitate to bless someone else or see them in their highest light. It's not a good idea, however, to hold our friends with our will or limit their free will in any way. We must always remain unattached and allow them to express themselves however they choose to do so.

Attachment contradicts Oneness. Essentially, we attach ourselves to others because we desire to have some control over how they live their lives. We're afraid that, left to their own devices, they would abandon us. Ultimately, all of this works against us and works against our coming together in true Oneness. Our desire to control has created an "us vs. them" scenario. We've subtly fabricated yet another way to separate ourselves.

There is also another big drawback to being attached - it opens a space for suffering to occur. Most people don't realize that *attachment is the only thing that brings about sorrow and suffering.* It helps us immensely if we understand that when we attach ourself to someone else (or something else), we inherently create a scenario whereby we set ourself up for a loss. We run the risk of losing them. However, if, in our relationships, we let others go from the very beginning, we'll find that we have nothing to lose, and suffering can't occur.

Suffering isn't necessary, and it never helps anyone. It only takes away from our energy and the energy of those around us. We needn't be in sorrow for any reason whatsoever. We are here on this beautiful, abundant Earth to live our life as a light and to keep our light burning brightly for all to see.

Those who are living in their highest light know that it is good to share your life and your love, for we have, indeed, come together for a reason. Feel free to fill your days and nights with love for your partner, your family, your friends, your pets, your possessions and everything, for these are all gifts unto you. Just remember that it is unwise to let your attachment to anyone or anything take one minute away from your joy.

Granting A Full Pardon

Consider this scenerio: You've hurt someone. Perhaps you didn't mean to do it - or perhaps you did. You may have just hurt their feelings a little bit, or you may have harmed their body and caused them considerable pain. In either case, for some inexplicable reason, you've decided to take a closer look at things and now you want to make amends.

You go to approach them, not knowing what to expect, but thinking about how you would like them to react to you. Wouldn't it be great if they said, "I completely forgive you. Don't concern yourself with me; just go on and enjoy your life as if nothing happened."

That is the way most people would like to be treated. And yet, it's standard operating procedure in our society to hold a grudge or seek revenge. Many would say that it's a natural human response for us to strike back. This is not so, but one thing is certain: We are constantly conditioned by our media to be vengeful. The media is a very powerful hypnotist, suggesting to us from early childhood that we must demand an "eye for an eye". Almost half of the movies out there today follow this theme. So we shouldn't be surprised when we find ourselves seeking revenge in real life.

There are many, however, who prefer to take a higher road. They know that revenge comes back to haunt, while the compassionate granting of a full pardon sets an example that leads to peace. In fact, many roads other than revenge offer themselves to us. One of the highest is to see all events and experiences as perfect. Everything is just as it should be. There is no wrongdoing - *only lessons that take us to a greater awareness.* Those who walk this road have transcended forgiveness. They live in a state of "Isness" and, from their perspective, there's no need to pardon someone who hasn't done anything wrong in the first place.

For others who tend to carry their hurt for awhile, another high road presents itself: Seeing themselves in the other person. When we realize that we are all One, and that the Spiritual Being who resides in another's body is the same Being who resides in ours, we cannot help but forgive. For who among us would seek revenge against themselves?

In actual practice, when some people first hear about these teachings, they have a challenging time looking at others in their highest light. They still see a lot of wrongdoing in the world, but don't know what to do about it. If you're in this group, another alternative is available to you. The next time you feel like someone else has treated you badly - for no reason other than to see what will happen - go to them and tell them that you forgive them unconditionally. Don't worry about how they will react. It's not their reaction that's important. It's what occurs inside of you that matters.

If your pardon is true and sincere (and especially if you've also forgiven yourself), you'll feel a wonderful relaxation in your midsection and a newfound freedom from the tension that was there before. You'll feel like you just swallowed a powerful magic potion that cured all of your ills.

And you'll want more of it.

*It is for yourself
that you see others in their highest light*

The Story Of Another Christ

Many of you will achieve being One with your Higher Self in this lifetime. Here is a very special story about a great warrior general who showed the way.

This man was the commander-in-chief of vast armies in a time which has long been forgotten in our current reckoning of history. He was both respected and feared as one of the most powerful men in the realm. At the time our tale begins, two great civilizations known as Atlantis and Lemuria had been involved in a series of wars for centuries, and, despite all efforts to bring peace to the land, no one of integrity had stepped forward to speak out on behalf of the true good of the people. The world situation was at a stalemate; a cycle of decadence and darkness prevailed.

Envision, if you will, a setting late one autumn afternoon toward the end of a particularly bloody battle in a valley that was strewn with bodies of brave men and women. With no sign of either side looking to retreat, the carnage continued unabated. The commander of the Lemurian army had fought relentlessly all day alongside his fellow soldiers and his sword was covered with the blood and sinew of fallen enemies. Though weary and wounded, he battled on, willing to fight until the last man was left standing or he himself was killed.

At a certain moment, with the twilight fast approaching, he found himself in a furious struggle with a very strong, courageous opponent. After almost 20 minutes of toe-to-toe combat against this formidable warrior, the Lemurian commander swung his mighty sword at his rival and connected. The brave man fell on his back, his helmet and sword flew to the ground beside him. Just as the great commander readied to run his sword through the defenseless man's chest, he paused for an instant to look into the face of his enemy. The soldier was just a boy - no more than 17 or 18 years of age - whose body had matured rapidly considering its years. The young man's eyes were filled with a terror beyond imagination; he knew that he was about to die.

Suddenly, as often happens when one is pushed to the limits of strength and endurance, the great commander's perception shifted. With his sword held high in the air, he glanced out of the corner of his eye at the bloody battle that raged around him. Arms and legs flailed in a strange slow motion-like dance, nearby shouts and screams seemed to come from far off in the distance. His entire awareness changed as a new power rippled through his body. He felt expanded into something much greater than he was just moments before. In that same instant, his knowledge increased dramatically - the future and past revealed themselves in one momentous flash. He looked down at the boy laying at his feet and saw into the depths of his young opponent's soul. This boy didn't want to die. He longed to be safe and warm in the comforts of his own home with his loved ones and family. He dreamt of once again running through the fields with the beautiful fiancée he left behind when he went off to war.

The great commander then saw of a part of himself in the young man's eyes; he saw a part of himself in everything around him. A feeling of deep compassion, such as he had never known before, overcame him. He knew he could not move to kill the helpless boy because, in doing so, he would only be killing himself. He dropped his sword to the ground and walked away from the battle to the top of a nearby hill.

What happened next was told and retold, passed on

from generation to generation for thousands of years. There, as darkness shrouded the land, he fell to his knees, vowing never to harm or kill again. . . and in that moment, he was enlightened. Immediately, the soldiers in the valley below stopped their fighting and looked to the glow on the hill. Ten thousand people witnessed the light as it became brighter and brighter and broke free from its connection with the Earth. The great commander slowly ascended to perhaps 300 feet above the hill and then gently floated to a point directly over the center of the battlefield. Some said that he hovered there for only a short time, while others reported that it seemed like hours. However long it was, all of those present were bathed and purified in the crystal blue-white radiance that gently showered down on them from above. None who were there that evening would ever go forth to fight again. Mercy and a new respect for one's fellow man were reborn within the human experience.

In time, the hovering white light began to fade and an outline of the commander's body took shape again. He settled slowly to the Earth and beckoned the soldiers to step back and give him room. Directly, he approached the boy who had fallen defenseless beneath his sword earlier and held out his arms. The two embraced like long-lost brothers, and when they finally pulled apart, the great commander bid the boy to go home to his family and fiancée and live his life in peace.

As the story goes, all of the soldiers on both sides left their weapons laying on the ground that night and sat around campfires together in silence. The next morning they began their return home to their families, carrying with them the story of what had happened the day before. Word quickly spread far and wide of a new Savior who walked the land. The great commander had become a Christed Being, a warrior for the light, and, from that point on, everywhere he went people were transformed, as if by magic, into fulfilled, joyful human beings. The series of wars that had lasted for centuries came to a sudden halt. Atlantis and Lemuria flourished once again as they had before the senseless wars had started.

It would be another 13,000 years before mankind forgot about the power of mercy and the example that was set that night by the great commander. These two magnificent cultures and all of their wondrous architectural and scientific achievements would one day be washed beneath the ocean waves into the sea and lost forever. But that is not the end of our tale.

The great commander/Savior's teachings, after being forgotten for lifetimes upon lifetimes, are now returning to the people of the Earth. His messages are heard in quiet moments in the minds of those who call forth the return of mercy. More and more people each day are choosing to lay down their swords and set aside their control issues in favor of peace. More and more are urging their national leaders to stop bullying one another and take a stance for the highest interests of all mankind. We are beginning to understand that acts of compassion and mercy inherently vanquish fear and return us to safety and comfort. We are moving toward a better world.

Furthermore, it is now being heralded, in obscure writings here and there, that the great ascended commander himself will return one day in the near future to walk again among the people and show them the magnificent rewards that come to the merciful. Indeed, among the scribes who announce his return, there is one man who has faint memories - visions - of a lifetime long past when he lay, defeated and helpless, on his back with a great warrior standing over him, sword raised and ready to strike. And sometimes, in rare moments of even deeper contemplation, he remembers a pact made between his soul and the soul of the great commander. Their agreement was to come to Earth in times of unrelenting darkness and play out the roles of courageous rivals so that this message about the power of mercy could be given unto you.

Healing Others

Along with seeing others in their highest light, having compassion is necessary in order to bring about a healing in someone else's life. Compassion - the strong desire to alleviate the suffering of your fellow man and woman - is to the feminine what mercy is to the masculine. Compassion calls forth our feelings, allowing us to identify with the emotional, as well as the physical challenges of another. Without it, true healing cannot occur.

As with healing oneself, there are several steps to be followed. A healer must first get the permission of the imbalanced person before proceeding. This is done by asking if they really want to be healed. In addition, the imbalanced person must also indicate that they truly believe that the healing will work. If they are doubtful or skeptical, then everyone is wasting their time. But if they are sincere, and give their permission, then true healing is possible. (Please note that one of the reasons that healers seek permission is so that they will know that they are not being manipulative. It doesn't serve anyone to force their own beliefs or behaviors on someone else, for in doing so, they would be attempting to control others. True white light healers do not seek to control, but to love.)

Assuming at this point that you have permission, your heart is open, and you are truly compassionate, you will now need to be in close communication with the Living Universe. It is this connection which creates a pathway for refined healing energies to flow from the Universe through the healer and into the person who is in need of assistance. In essence, the healer only acts as a catalyst, a go-between between the Universe and the imbalanced person. Those who are not meditating or praying on a consistent basis will not be as able to make the connection that is required to effectively heal another.

Just as the healer needs to connect with the Universe, he or she must also maintain a firm connection with the Earth during a healing. If the healer is not properly grounded, residual energies that have abandoned the body of the healed person may attempt to lodge themselves in the body of the healer. This cannot happen, however, if the healer has established a firm connection between the Universe and the Earth. A conduit must be created which sends all of the residual energies directly into the ground.

It is also important to understand that healers do not usually carry around a reservoir of healing energies of their own which are accumulated and then depleted during a healing session. Those who say that they feel drained or uncomfortable after a healing have probably not taken the time to properly ground themselves. By the same token, healers who are able to hold a strong connection between Heaven and Earth during the healing process are much more apt to feel recharged and rejuvenated than depleted after a session.

Now let's do a quick recap of the healing process. In order to heal another, we must:

1.) Be compassionate
2.) Have their permission
3.) Invoke the healing power of the Universe
4.) Stay grounded
5.) See them in their highest light

This last step - seeing them in their highest light - is where the magic actually takes place. As we picture them in their highest light - happy, healthy and healed - we do for them what they have been unable to do for themselves. To the extent that we hold that vision while maintaining a strong connection between Heaven and Earth, our thoughts will begin to coagulate, become denser and denser, and the physical body will have no choice but to respond. In accordance with the laws of manifestation, balance will be restored. Light replaces dark and disease disappears. Now the person who was once imbalanced can go forth, expressing life fully and freely, into a new and brighter day.

Recently, I heard a good story about a lady named Barbara who went down to Brazil to see a healer. At the time, Barbara didn't have anything in particular wrong with her that she knew of. She just wanted to experience this wonderful man's presence. For the first two weeks that she was there, most of her days were spent in group meditations. She was feeling great, but was also beginning to wonder about what was going on with the healer, when one morning he came into the room and asked her and the 50 or 60 other people who were there to remain silent for a few moments. Then he held his hand up toward the audience and waved it in a slow arching motion for a short time and left.

Barbara immediately noticed a slight tickle above her waist, so she reached down and pulled up her blouse to see what it was. To her surprise, there were several stitches in her side that weren't there before. It was clear that something had been removed, just as if she'd been in surgery. What it was, she didn't know. Nor did she have any idea how the stitches got there. She was sure, however, that she'd been healed.

III.

- Lighting Up The Earth -
Seeing Our World In Its Highest Light

Our Next Step Together

These magnificent times we live in have it all - the good guys, the bad guys, a spurious system of time, a dubious semblance of history, ever-expanding communications capabilities, money shortages, hidden truths, and personal challenges galore. Out of all of the possible experiences throughout the Universe that we could have chosen to involve ourselves in, there is none more extraordinary, more momentous, than living here on Earth in this generation. We are rare, courageous Spirits, all of us, and we are not without purpose at this time of great transition. We are here because we have the strength and ability to make a difference in how our evolution proceeds.

Let us begin this segment of our teachings with a short exploration into the nature of time. At present, people worldwide agree that the Julian Calendar works just fine. Few question how it got here or if it actually benefits the human race. Most know that it was created a little over 2000 years ago by the leader of the Holy

Roman Empire, Julius Caesar. Yet little attention has been paid to the changes that have been made along the way - most notably, ten days that were summarily subtracted by edict of Pope Gregory XIII in 1582. As long as we get to work on time and our paychecks are in the slot on Friday, we rarely take into consideration that our clocks and calendars are obvious constructs designed to keep us controlled.

Those who are curious enough to seek out a credible system of time need not look too far. The Mayans left a legacy which puts all other time constructs to shame. The Mayan Calendar, at its core, encompasses a vastly larger cosmology than the Julian calendar. It reflects the precise movements of the heavenly bodies which surround us. No discussion of mankind's next step would be complete without reference to it.

Since long before the influence of the Holy Roman Empire, the Mayans appointed responsible individuals to chart and intuit the movements of the cosmos. These people, whom they called "the keepers of time" passed their findings from parent to child, generation to generation, thus keeping an accurate system of time measurement alive. Despite persistent efforts made by those who would bury and banish the legacy of the Mayans, "the keepers of time" kept the flame of truth burning brightly, deep within the forests and jungles of Central America. We owe these remarkable people a debt of gratitude as we approach this unique juncture in history. It is because of them that we are gifted with an incomparable guideline that will help us all to evolve.

To put everything into perspective, let's take a look at a brief description of our current situation according to the Mayans. They tell us that there are several very large cosmological cycles coming to completion at the same time. Just as our Earth revolves around our Sun every year, so does our solar system revolve around a much brighter sun called Alcyone every 26,000 years. And, likewise, that entire system revolves around the center of our galaxy, the Milky Way, every 230 million years. The Milky Way is also in constant motion. It is in an infinitely larger orbital pattern around the Great Central Sun of the Universe. All three of these great cycles - the solar system cycle of 26,000 years, the Alcyone cycle of 230 million years, and the Milky Way cycle which covers an infinitely larger timespan - will synchronistically come to their evolutionary completion all at the same moment in the year 2012 AD.

Considering that all of these great cycles are coordinated to converge in 2012, and that we are somehow affected in a positive way, it might be wise for us to see what we can do to help facilitate this giant evolutionary leap.

First, and foremost, we must learn to see all events that occur in their highest light. Regardless of what is happening around us, we must remember that there is an opportunity in all experiences and that we have the inherent ability to sail through any challenges smoothly if we maintain our focus on the highest perspective. If others choose to complain or fret during these times of great change, it is up to us to remain steadfast and hold a vision that serves ourselves and our world. This is how we evolve.

Second, we must free ourselves from the manipulations of the Self-Appointed World Managers - those who currently pull the puppet strings of mankind. In order to do this, we'll need to peek around in the dark a little bit because the SAWM plan and scheme from places where we cannot easily see them. The boardrooms of the international bankers, the castles in the Swiss Alps, and the lavish, guarded living quarters of the upper echelons of the SAWM are not splashed across the pages of People Magazine. Secrets, however, are always revealed at their source; therefore, one only needs to follow the world's money supply to its source in order to find out who the Self-Appointed World Managers are.

Without naming names, we will say that these men are the ones who propagate fear and do everything in their power to keep people from reaching their highest potential. They keep mankind perpetually off balance and under pressure by the measured administration of wars, diseases, media manipulations, monetary restraints, mediocre-level leadership, limited educational information, and so on. Those who oppose the SAWM are often ridiculed and scandalized, leaving the truth to be exiled to out-of-the-way places, except for one - *within us*. The SAWM can do everything in their power to get inside our minds and impose the consensus reality upon us, but, ultimately, the choices we make are up to us.

People today generally tend to buy into the consensus reality that is presented to them on the television. They believe everything from the latest political gyrations to the weather, not realizing that these are constructs which are suggested to them. The time has come when we must decide, in each and every instance, if the suggestion we're presented with is one which serves us or one which does not serve us. Of course, it's simple to follow along with the crowd and not rock the boat. But if we're going to create a new paradigm and live in a peaceful world, it might be wise to begin a little boat-rocking.

The best place to start is in our own thoughts and words. We can reject the consensus reality, and when someone asks, "Who are you going to vote for?", we can choose to answer, "No one, because I am my own leader. I'm not harming anybody and I don't want to support anyone who doesn't really care about me." Similarly, if a friend reports, "There's a new virus going around", we can respond, "I don't choose to use my healthy body for sickness or disease." Likewise, whenever a frightened neighbor says "There are enemies approaching who are threatening our way of life," a good reply is, "I don't play the 'us versus them' separation game. I know that when I take a defensive posture, I'm actually drawing an attack to me. And besides that, I'm working to bring <u>all</u> human beings together into one big happy family!"

Soon there will be enough individuals who have the inner strength to envision a new reality and to discard that which is told to them by others who do not have their best interests at heart. The important battles are not waged on foreign soil, but in the hearts and minds of courageous individuals. If we are to live in peace, we must think and speak only of peace. Any other behavior continues to reinforce conflict. By the same token, if we are to live in good health, we must think and speak only of wellness. Any other behavior reinforces that which makes us sick. And so it is with all attributes which we desire to manifest.

These are the times for more people to understand that reinforcing our old ways will only continue to penalize us and lead to further struggle and strife. We are living on the cusp of a critical juncture, according to the Mayans, which summons us to begin thinking and speaking of ourselves only in our highest light. When enough of us are responding according to the deepest calling of our soul, we will step together as One into a glorious new world.

Then we will truly be free.

There is no reason, whatsoever, why every human being who walks this Earth couldn't be given everything that he or she needs. Scarcity, in all of its insidious forms, can be tucked neatly away into our past and replaced by abundance beyond measure. Oppression can give way to a life of total freedom such as we have never before experienced. And fear can now be seen for what it truly is - a cry in the dark for attention, a call for the gift of comfort and peace.

For as that loving attention is freely given without reservation, a light so bright will shine forth on everyone and everything. The streets will be filled with people smiling at each other, wanting one and all to experience the joy that comes when we live our lives to the fullest. Everywhere you look there will be peace. We are cleansed of all impurity by the Living Universe as It surrounds us and bathes us in the Highest Light imaginable. Once again we are innocent as young babes, yet divinely empowered, and thrilled at the wonders that lie before us.

Peace Must Take Precedence

Patriotism is the great divider. It discourages individual empowerment, while advocating blame. It distracts common sense, while inciting anger. And, to our great loss, it disavows Oneness while propagating pain and suffering. It bids us to resolve our differences by killing our fellowman. There can be no doubt that the human race would be immeasurably better off if we were to cast all patriotic movements aside and take our chances with any of the other alternatives.

The mechanics of patriotism are simple: Keep people separated from each other by any means necessary and tell them that the other guys are out for their blood. Throw in a few rumors of food and gasoline shortages, set the flags to waving, play the marching music loud, and feed in the fear factor on the nightly news. After that, all you have to do is turn a few hired fanatics loose with guns and they'll do the rest. For patriotism is an emotional outlet. It plays upon those who make decisions from their emotions, without paying much attention to their thoughts. Thinking people are much less likely to endorse conflict and patriotic solutions because they can see the inherent good in coming together. They see the benefit in building bridges instead of tearing them down.

We would all be well served to remember that our worldly experiences take place in our minds long before we act them out in our daily lives. Whatever thoughts a person dwells upon, that's what he or she is going to manifest.

To use our defense mindset as an example, *when you're thinking that someone else is going to attack you, you are actually helping to create that attack*. A defensive position always invites an attack. It works like this: In your mind, you're picturing someone - perhaps it's an enemy footsoldier, a renegade terrorist, or a drugged-out street criminal - coming to get you. This is a thought, just like all other thoughts. With enough attention put on it, it will work its way toward the surface of your experience, just like the thought that you're going to go to Disneyland next month.

Fortunately, we can pick any thought we want. Thoughts that serve us and those that don't are equally available to us. If a person envisions attackers, then he will be attacked. If a person envisions Disneyland, then he'd better get his E tickets ready. The question is: What kind of world do we want to live in? If we keep envisioning the same old "us vs. them" separation scenerios as propagated by the powermoguls' media, then we'll never live in peace. But, if we shed our victim mentality and begin to picture our world in its highest light, then things will change. Thousands of years of man killing his fellowman will come to an end and be replaced by the expression of a deep and abiding respect for one another. All it takes is a little deeper thinking. We must stop letting those with their own personal agendas tell us who our enemies are. We must investigate a little further to discover who the true perpetrators of violence on this planet are. And we must reject their manipulative suggestions and begin to discern in favor of that which is for the highest good of all.

For those who want to live in true freedom (not the kind of freedom offered by most present-day patriotic movements), peace needs to take the highest precedence. We must, in fact, demand peace because freedom requires a peaceful environment in which to grow and thrive. As of yet, not enough of us have been able to garner the inner strength needed to create a lasting peace. There are a few - and more are seeing the light every day - but it takes a larger number of people to stop supporting a social reality that doesn't serve them before a shift into true collective sovereignty will occur.

To put it another way, the world nowadays needs more warriors for peace; people who realize that solutions sought on the battlefield will not provide results that work on our behalf. The true battlefield, as we said earlier, does not stretch out across blood-drenched soils or campus lawns, but is in our own hearts and minds. When enough people begin to put away all patriotic thoughts and envision our world in its highest light, then we will, at long last, be at peace.

It starts out with a few courageous souls who declare themselves free, and who are willing to live that ideal for all the world to see. Then a few more will glean the wisdom of being their own sovereign authority. Not long after that, a larger mass will find their inner balance and reclaim that which belongs to them. And finally, our entire worldview shifts as all human beings who walk this Earth stand united as One, dedicated to allowing people everywhere to live their lives in absolute freedom. That is the key to realizing our highest potential - and we must hold onto it and pamper it as if it is the greatest gift in our possession.

The time will come, in our very near future, when one more person envisions a peaceful world and, with that seemingly tiny action, the scales are tipped. The storm clouds disappear and a new world, the world that we deserve to live in as our right of birth, opens up before us.

It will be like a miracle ... but it's not really a miracle. It's only us having changed our thoughts.

The Good Side

The law that our thoughts create our experiences is not just a law unto each isolated individual. It is just as applicable to our collective beliefs. It only takes a certain number of us to see our world in its highest light before it will manifest for all of us. To say it another way, when enough people are able to hold a vision of a new, peaceful world, the human race, *in its entirety*, will begin to experience paradise on Earth.

And then, there's the icing on the cake. It can happen fast. It can happen in our lifetimes. We need not think that we are only making things better for future generations. We are also making things better for ourselves. It can start with the smallest spark, and, quick as a wink, it can spread around the entire globe.

One place to begin is by seeing <u>all</u> others in their highest light - even the international bankers and powermoguls who have used deceit and fear in order to maintain control over us. We so often forget that each man, no matter how bad we think he is, does have, without exception, a good guy deep down inside. To remember this and to act accordingly is one of the biggest challenges facing mankind today.

For some reason - perhaps because of our own desire to dominate others - we have overlooked our ability to see the good side of the SAWM. We don't often envision him in his highest light. Unfortunately, if we don't acknowledge his good side, he'll continue to ride roughshod over us. However, when we see all people, including our puppeteers, in their highest light, they will eventually mirror our visions of them.

Something very magical takes place within our opponents when we see them in their highest light. Whenever they are confronted by someone who sets a noble example, they undergo a measurable change in their psyche, a chemical organic rearrangement that is accompanied by a softening of the heart. It may be subtle at first, but it will touch them, just as when you chip away at a large rock. After awhile, it turns into a pile of small stones - or a statue of great beauty.

Walls of separation dissolve as the SAWM begins to follow our example and seeks for his own highest light inside himself. His heart opens and his mind recognizes the wisdom in becoming One with others. In his newfound perspective, he will find a world that is better than the one in which he spent all of his energy trying to control everything and everyone around him. He'll experience a feeling of great joy that was unavailable to him as long as he exploited others.

And from that point on, we'll all be much happier because, instead of continuing to deal with the challenges of getting along with each other, we can all start to work together on the challenges of how we make our world as good as it can possibly be.

Every one of us is seen and known for who we truly are at the depths of our Being

Live Wires Make Great Connections

Many of you are catalysts. In the times to come you will have a lot to do with communities and getting people together so that they can help each other. There are many groups scattered around the Earth who do not know that others like themselves even exist. In your travels, you're going to help to bring them together so they'll know about each other and know about each other's good works.

You will find these grassroots groups to be as small as a handful of dedicated people or as large as a community of thousands. They will go by many different names; some may call themselves Intenders of the Highest Good, while others call themselves The Garden Club. It doesn't matter what they're named as long as they're open and following some sort of positive, uplifting belief system.

People always benefit from finding out what other people have done. It isn't necessary to remake the wheel every time we turn around. There are people in Greenpeace and the Audubon Society and the Sierra Club and many, many more who are working hard to preserve our precious environment. There are amazing connections from Virginia Beach to the Four Corners to Mount Shasta who are exploring the highest potentials of the human being. They all have something wonderful to share with you. You can visit these groups and take the lessons that you have learned back to your own community.

And there is the Internet. It is full of people who are ready to help you. It abounds with talk of new ideas that wouldn't otherwise come to the surface in the mainstream media. You can go into a search engine and, in a matter of seconds, find out about everything from free energy sources to meditation techniques. It's all there, and, as long as it remains unregulated by those who would seek to control others, it will bring more and more freedom into our lives.

If you are part of a community and you find yourself traveling around the countryside or browsing the World Wide Web, know that wherever you are, there is a message there for you. Sometimes you may have to pay very close attention, but be assured that you can learn something valuable from whatever you are doing. Then you can keep the flow going by sharing it with others.

Every community needs its catalysts, its live wires. *It's easy to tell these live wires by their connections.* When it's time for your group to spread its wings, you will have connected with people who've already been through what you're going through. They will help you and you will help them. You will become a part of them, and they'll become a part of you. And, pretty soon, we will have all come together in the name of abundance and peace and harmony for all mankind.

Know that you are assisting others
by your own realizations
You then enhance and increase the possibilities
for others to go where you have been

The Highest Light Party

Get-togethers can be a lot of fun. Since mankind came to this Earth, the sharing of food and socializing have been a means for people to connect and uplift each other. In times past, those in more advanced societies knew the wisdom in spending a part of their evening for higher purposes. People would chat, laugh, and eat together for awhile, but, before they went home, they would always take time to sit in a circle and make a connection with the Highest Light. This guaranteed that they would leave the gathering feeling good.

Today's partygoers tend to forget about this ancient tradition. Socializing nowadays often centers around immoderate eating and drinking, while the subject matter of the typical conversation has degenerated considerably. In forgetting that our words have a very direct impact on our lives, many of today's socialites easily slip into talking about worst-case scenarios, and, therefore, they create experiences that are not very comfortable for themselves.

How often have you been at a party and found yourself gabbing about the poor economy, the chances of war, a new flu that's going around, or somebody else's problems? No one even stops to consider that, by discussing these discomforting subjects, you and your friends are actually reinforcing and manifesting them. As the evening wears on, a kind of sluggishness sets in.

Later, when you arrive back at home, a little more tipsy than you'd like, you fall into bed wishing that you didn't feel so bad.

For those who have "been there and done that" and are looking for something different, we offer a wonderful alternative: a Highest Light party. All you have to do is get a few of your like-hearted friends together and first agree that you're only going to talk about things that feel good. Everybody can bring a dish so that you can share food, but leave the alcoholic beverages for another time. Your main focus is to eat, laugh a lot, and have a good time.

The last hour or so of the party can be set aside for something very special. You may follow any agenda that's comfortable for you and your friends, but, during this time, it's important that everyone sits in a circle. Perhaps you might want to start out by having a short meditation or prayer to set the mood. Or you could chant and drum or sing together for a little while. It doesn't matter how you raise your Spirits, just as long as you do.

Now you've set the stage for magic and miracles to happen. It's time for each one of you to take a few minutes and share your visions of a better world. If you were living in your highest light, how would that look to you? If your world was shining its highest light, what would you see all around you? Don't hold back or limit yourselves. All things are possible. Know that in this sharing, you are being creative - you are bringing your grandest visions to life.

When everyone in the circle has had an opportunity to express themselves fully, you can stand-up, hold hands, and call in the Highest Light in the Universe. Ask that your visions serve the highest and best interests of all concerned, and then sound a harmonious tone for a few moments. After that, it's best to be silent and look within while the Universe works its magic.

When you're all complete, look around you at the smiles on the faces of your friends. Hug each other if you like. You can always be assured that after a party like this, you'll go home feeling great. And in the process, you will have contributed, perhaps more than you know, to the upliftment of your entire world.

Surround yourself with people who are supportive of where you are in your life now

Healing Our World

Our new world is reaching out to us in the same measure that we reach out to it. It is up to us to rise to the call and move forward into that which gloriously awaits us. We do this by abandoning our old ways, while stretching our imagination to its limits. And there is one more thing: We must trust. The laws of manifestation simply do not work if we do not trust in them. *It is the hallmark of this time in history that we are called upon to trust at a much deeper level that we have ever trusted before.* Building our trust is much like building a muscle in our body. The more we exercise it or put it to work, the stronger it gets. It doesn't take long, especially in these times of accelerated evolution, before our trust will turn into a knowing - a knowing that we are all-powerful, masterful creators whose time has come.

When one is trusting in the innate goodness of the Universe, it's easy to give up our old ways of doing things. Our reliance upon everything from poor leadership to destructive energy sources melts away in the light of new, more pleasing alternatives. There are those, of course, who will cry out that the transition will be too rough; that if they were to let go of their present way of life, there wouldn't be enough food on the table or there wouldn't be a roof over their heads. In short, they're unable to envision a way to step into the new paradigm that doesn't threaten their current security and survival belief systems.

To these people, our response is always the same: *Seek self-empowerment.* You can have complete control over your life. Others cannot dictate your reality to you unless you let them. By your thoughts, you create your world. And you can choose to change it all.

Each and every person on this beautiful, magnificent Earth can, with a little practice, become self-empowered. Indeed, food, shelter, and all good things can be manifested if only one trusts in the laws of creation. The fears that have been running our lives for eons are but shadows of the truth. They always cower and shrink when we take heart and allow our Spirits to come forth. No one need suffer, ever. Self empowerment - *the ability to easily manifest that which we desire* - is available to all for the asking.

Once we've taken heart and learned to trust in our power, the next step is to stretch our imagination and know that we can create anything that we can think of. When we go beyond the bounds of our old, consensus reality, whole new realms open up before us. We can have leaders who are kind and beneficent; we can clean our air and water in a matter of days; we can enjoy free energy, free food, free shelter, free everything! A life of total comfort is available to anyone who is willing to shed their old thinking processes. Let's take a look at an example of this to see how it works.

Almost everyone in our world today believes that we are at the mercy of the weather. The weatherman comes on the nightly news and tells us that a terrible storm is on the way, and we think that there's nothing we can do about it. Since enough people believe in the authority of the friendly weatherman, we begin to spread his gospel to those around us and, in doing so, we are actually helping to create the inclement weather. In other words, a lot of people, working together, have a lot of power. If they choose to believe in the promptings of someone else (in this case, the TV weatherman), then, as you can see, their beliefs will work against them.

If, on the other hand, people begin to realize that they can come together and create a more comfortable experience for themselves, then that is what will happen. Weather conditions are no exception. We can dissolve the clouds, bring the rains, or move the storms around us, if only we believe we can. The ancients were good at this and didn't hesitate to create comfortable weather. They took advantage of the fullness of their imagination. And they worked closely together for the benefit of the whole group. We can do the same.

The weather is but one small example. Our environment, in all its wondrous manifestations, has the potential for great change. *It is alive and ready, at a moment's notice, to respond to our direction and work with us to co-create purity, beauty, and abundance beyond measure.* The key is for more of us to hold a vision that serves not just the few, but everyone involved.

Many visions avail themselves to us and many offer great rewards. Our choices are limitless. There is one vision, however, that serves us infinitely better than all the rest. The Highest Light. It is the closest thing that we have to a magic wand. When enough of us choose to see our world in its Highest Light, everything will be different. We'll automatically bring about a healing such as we have never before enjoyed in the entire history of mankind.

*You can have anything and everything
you could possibly dream of -
even a whole new world to live in*

IV.

- The Light Of A Thousand Suns - Seeing The Universe In Its Highest Light

All roads eventually lead inward to their source. The only way to prolong our outer experience is to turn our back on the Universe. The Universe, in Its infinite love and wisdom gives us free will to express ourselves in any way we choose. If we decide to work closely with It, then we can be assured of Its cooperation. By the same token, if we choose to shake our fist in anger at It, proclaiming that our life is a mess and that there's nothing we can do about it, the Universe will also comply by seeing to it that we experience our disempowerment.

To put it another way, the Universe always provides us with the experiences that we ask for. If we supply It with a positive direction, we access our power and all good things. If we do not choose to consciously communicate with the Universe, then anything goes. We open ourselves up to all sorts of experiences that do not serve us or bring us comfort. We abdicate our power, thus allowing others whose motives may be selfish to have dominion over us. It's not the fault of the Universe if we are suffering. By our own reluctance to furnish It with positive guidelines, we bring suffering unto ourselves.

So now, let's turn the tables on our suffering and scarcity and look on the bright side by exploring how we can take the above information and put it to good use in our lives. The secret to our greatest happiness lies in our seeing the Universe in Its Highest Light. All things become possible when we acknowledge the highest attributes of our Supreme Creator. We can easily gain access to infinite kindness, helpfulness, mercy, freedom, abundance, wisdom, compassion, peace, love, and all things beneficial. All we have to do is break down our old inner barriers and speak directly to the Living Universe. We must give It positive directions.

Each and every one of us can experience what it's like to dwell in the Highest Light. Not one who asks shall be denied. All who step forth, with trust and love in their hearts, are answered. The Universe wants you to know your power. It wants you to have it all. Indeed, It longs to stop your suffering and waits for the moment when you will approach in earnest so that It can show you the fullest expression of yourself. The Source of who you are constantly shines Its Highest Light as a beacon and steps within an inch, bidding you to enter Its sweet embrace.

The next step, however, is up to you.

Take a deep breath or two, suspend your old beliefs for a moment, and call forth the Living Essence of the Universe. Relax and allow it to settle in . . .

Feel a soothing warmth come into your body and spread throughout your limbs. Let it fill your every cell with light and then expand out past the edges of your skin into the surrounding air. Extend it outward even farther so that you are encapsulated by a glow of soft, rejuvenating light that holds you in sheer comfort.

Now envision this wonderful light infusing you with all of the highest attributes of the Universe Itself. Call in all-wisdom, all-power, love for all creation. Call in abundance, mercy, kindness, compassion, grace, freedom, harmony, and peace beyond any peace you have ever felt before. Touch the heart of the Living Universe and allow It to pull you in. Let its highest attributes become yours. Let its wisdom be your wisdom. Let its power be your power. Let its love be your love.

Breathe even deeper now and express your heartfelt gratitude for all of the magnificent gifts that the Universe is offering. Allow yourself to be lifted up to the peak of human experience. Feel, to the very core of your Being, your complete and utter joy spreading and joining you together with all and everything you see.

You are One with your fellow travelers.
You are One with your world.
You are One with The Highest Light.

You are One

How To Order From Us

1. Call us tollfree at 1-888-422-2420
2. Visit our website at www.intenders.com
3. Send your order with a check or M.O. to:

The Intenders
PO Box 1491 Corrales, NM 87048

THE INTENDERS HANDBOOK
A Guide to the Intention Process
and the Conscious Community
$4.00 + $1.00 S & H

THE INTENDERS OF THE HIGHEST GOOD
Novel by Tony Burroughs
$14.95 + $4.00 S & H

THE INTENDERS VIDEO
The Intention Process:
A Guide for Conscious Manifestation
and Community-Making
$15.00 + $4.00 S & H

CREATE YOUR OWN COMMUNITY
Our Intenderpreneur Package Special
10 Intenders Handbooks + 1 Intenders Video
$33.00 + $6.00 S & H

THE HIGHEST LIGHT TEACHINGS
$4.95 + $1.00 S & H
(For orders of 10 or more, $3.00 each + S & H)